Traces Of Pain

Jaycie Maycock

BookLeaf
Publishing

India | USA | UK

Made with ❤ on the BookLeaf Publishing Platform
www.bookleafpub.in
www.bookleafpub.com

Dedication

To: ....

(Insert name above)

Preface

Dear Readers,

Thank you for taking the time to journey through these pages with me. This collection is deeply personal, reflecting my experiences with trauma, depersonalization, and love to name a few. Each poem serves as a whisper of my innermost thoughts.

In sharing these pieces, I hope to illuminate the shadows and remind you that you are not alone in your struggles. Together, may we find solace and strength in our shared humanity.

With gratitude,

Jaycie Maycock

Acknowledgements

I would like to extend my heartfelt gratitude to Book Leaf Publishing for supporting my vision and making this collection a reality.

A special shoutout to all the incredible individuals who reached out to me during my hardest years. Your letters were beacons of hope, reminding me that I was never alone. Thank you for your kindness, encouragement, and for sharing your words with me.

On edge
A tingle down my spine
Like I'm walking in the dark
Someone following behind

I go through life
Waiting for him to show
Demand his daughter
Make his title known

Will the shoe drop
Or the rug be pulled
His absence has me
Deceptively lulled

He's still out there
So I stay cautious
I hold the evidence tight
Fear in my subconscious

Pressure heavy as rocks
Pouring from my eyes
My stomach in knots
Accepting the lies
This is our battle
I know I have to fight
But I found in my hand
A flag of pure white

Our connection tested
We thrive in hard times
Vulnerability present
Our souls intertwined
My confidence remains
We shall survive

When I see stars in the sky
I think of all the people that died
The souls left untouched
The bodies buried with tears
Decaying throughout the years
I picture their different laughs
As each night comes to pass
I ponder at what will remain
When my heart too shall refrain

Awoken by a bright eyed smile
along with a poke to the eye
"good morning starshine"

Pulling like I'm stuck in quicksand
I search my phone for a reply
I let the silence overtake my morning

Adding up the expenses
My mind starts to race
I now work where once treated

Entering another new home
One look and I'm needed again
Grasping onto me like a Venus fly trap

I blink, in an istant
A thought appears
Churns my stomach
Reveals my fears

I lose you, my love
we just drift apart
You leave me behind
Taking my heart

Though I assure myself
I will stay alive
Like a plant underwatered
I know I would not thrive

Behind my eyes
A cage there lies
With a full food plate
Of set daily intake
an untouched bottle
Water dripping from the nozzle
The wheel is spinning rough
But the hamster has fallen off
Not meeting the needs
Mental health depletes
I think "I need to be a better me"
Im focusing on the wrong things

The counters messy
The walls marked
The floors squeaked
Where generations walked
The door has a bell for the blind dog
A drawer filled with special nothings
A cookie jar with no cookies
A fridge marked with art
Grandmas kitchen Holds my heart

Their words move me to tears
Hold me all through the night
I remember all the years
They took away my fright

Thier words surround my walls
And persuade me to dance
They move me down the hall
Holding me in a trance

Their words a seed of hope
A beacon of light
a buoy with a rope
A guide to new sight

Their words frozen in time
yet forever moving
Just like flipping a dime
That never stops spinning

My fractured heart hurts me
Keeps me awake at night
My eyes burn from the insomnia
Now I cant trust anyone in sight
My legs may carry me places
But theres talk of them breaking down
I could be safe in this depression
Or I could just as easily drown

Cool breeze in my hair
Talk of night coming soon
She whispers to me

Dark begins to show
Just as it did yesterday
Night appears with grace

She calms the world
Sending children to sleep
Sounding the night owl

Such a beauy is she
I long to see her more
But she leaves me weary

Tucked away for safe keeping
I'm eager for you arrival
I'll continue to wait for your sake
Just know I think of you every day
I want to feel your tiny fingers in mine
And study the grooves of your face
But for now you just sleep tight
I love you my little pumpkin
Please dont go away

Here she stands with her quirky moles
I can see she feels out of control
She pulls at her stomach like pizza dough
Scanning the canvas up and down
Criticizing all of her flaws
Picking at her face in desperation
Ripping the hairs from her scalp

I want to grab her and show my love
All she is when she feels not enough
Her heart, laughter, and resilience,
What has made her so oblivious?
She is so harsh towards herself
It puts us both through hell
But I cannot offer protection
I am only her reflection

Suicide on the rise
Tears pour from my eyes
Absent mental state
I sit and contemplate
How many lives lost
What is the cause
The ones that survive
Gain a new sight on life
A change in perspective
On how were supposed to live
Take nothing for granted
Play the cards handed
Live life to the fullest
Check boxes off your list
We are all going to die
So why not enjoy the ride

Brain matter under my freshly painted nails
As I claw my way out of this mess
Disappointment at the situation
Im stuck in the filth consuming me
Eating me alive
I am jonah
My mind the whale
I refuse to turn to god

My consciousness sits
Behind my eyelid slits
Wiping at the gloss
Feeling so lost
She stares blankly around
No emotion found
Taking in her surrounding
Her body lacks belonging
Mind and body apart
Confusion in her heart
turning on the screen
Scroll through the feed
Be present she screams
Be the mom of your dreams
I feel a fog inside
I cannot comply

I met an artist
A curious creature
Filled me with hope
Gave me a picture
Took a brush and painted
The walls of my mind
Such an inspiration
He is one of a kind
This stranger of the hour
I was vulnerable to
Gave me the power
To do what I love to do
Ive been searching high and low
For the right motivation
Who knew that it could be found
In a dinner conversation

Death and I meet again
A chill runs down my spine
I can't unsee the imagery
A lulled tongue of the feline

The warm body implies recent
The fresh blood under confirms
The thought of the driver ignoring this
Is one that makes me squirm

The calm I feel when we kiss
Like walking through snowfall at night
my mind feels just as silent as when
I drive under a bridge in the pouring rain
Holding my breath and taking you in
Like being submerged under water
Almost as if i'm being sedated
Like waking but have yet to open my eyes

Seeing me as paper thin
Hands of stone laid on my skin
You painfully abused my trust
Losing a mentor Id have to adjust
As just a child I had to protect myself
Your actions are now filed on a shelf
I'm no longer under your lock
And that's how paper beats rock

The bright sun shines through
transformed by blue curtains
I drag myself outside to find
The fresh smell of overnight rain
I sink my bare toes into the grass
So damp it fills me with a rush
The sun is blinding as I try to spot
Birds that sang such a wonderful tune
And as I catch my breath I think
"This is what makes life worth living"